'LEGAL EMPOWERMENT OF THE POOR'
VERSUS 'RIGHT TO THE CITY'

IMPLICATIONS FOR ACCESS TO HOUSING
IN URBAN AFRICA

Louisa Vogiazides

NORDISKA AFRIKAINSTITUTET 2012

NAI Policy Dialogue is a series of short reports on policy relevant issues concerning Africa today. Aimed at professionals working within aid agencies, ministries of foreign affairs, NGOs and media, these reports aim to inform the public debate and to generate input in the sphere of policymaking. The writers are researchers and scholars engaged in African issues from several disciplinary points of departure. Most have an institutional connection to the Nordic Africa Institute or its research networks. The reports are internally endorsed and reviewed externally.

Indexing terms
Towns
Urban areas
Urbanization
Urban housing
Poverty
Low income groups
Property rights
Empowerment
Legislation
Research methods
Comparative analysis
Africa

Language checking: Peter Colenbrander
Cover photo: Jeronimo Giorgi, *Housing in Jos, Nigeria 2011*
ISSN 1654-6709
ISBN 978-91-7106-720-3
© The author and Nordiska Afrikainstitutet 2012
Production: Byrå4
Print on demand, Lightning Source UK Ltd.

Contents

List of abbreviations

AbM: Abahlali baseMjondolo
CLEP: Commission on Legal Empowerment of the Poor
FIFA: International Federation of Association Football
ILO: International Labour Organisation
LEP: Legal Empowerment of the Poor
NGO: Non-Governmental Organisation
SDI: Shack/Slum Dwellers International
UNDP: United Nations Development Programme
UNESCO: United Nations Educational, Scientific and
                 Cultural Organisation
UN-HABITAT: United Nations Human Settlements Programme

Abstract

This paper compares the major arguments found in the Legal Empowerment of the Poor (LEP) and the Right to the City discourses with particular reference to housing in urban Africa. After examining the major advocates, arguments and critiques associated with each discourse, it argues that they are based on two distinct sets of ideological and normative principles, with LEP being inspired by classical liberal ideas and Right to the City by Marxist thought. Consistent with these different ideological backgrounds, the two discourses have different views on access to housing in urban Africa, with LEP proposing ownership formalisation and market inclusion as a solution to lack of access to adequate and affordable housing, while Right to the City calls for increased state intervention in housing provision. The paper concludes, however, that the different ideological backgrounds do not necessarily mean their policy recommendations are incompatible, and calls for further research into the influence of the two discourses on housing policies in African cities.

Key words

Legal Empowerment, Right to the City, Africa, housing, informality, evictions, rights.

Foreword

Urban populations are growing rapidly in Africa as a result of both natural increase and migration from rural areas. There has been a longstanding concern in both academic and policy circles that an important proportion of urban residents face exclusion and limited access to basic resources. This Policy Dialogue discusses and contrasts two ideological formations that have gained ground internationally as diagnoses for and solutions to these problems: Legal Empowerment of the Poor and the Right to the City. It provides a rare comparison of these perspectives, and is a valuable contribution to policy analysis in the field of urban development. The author compares and contrasts the political ideologies that have inspired these perspectives and the different policy agendas they have given rise to. The analysis includes the ways in which each of the perspectives has evolved and been transformed as well as the critiques they have prompted. It continues with an illustration of how the two approaches have differently shaped policy agendas and discussions on access to housing in urban Africa.

This Policy Dialogue was written for the Urban Cluster of the Nordic Africa Institute in collaboration with the Department of Human Geography, Stockholm University. Its author, Louisa Vogiazides, has a master's degree from the latter department.

Jenny Cadstedt
Researcher
The Nordic Africa Institute

Ilda Lindell
Associate Professor
Department of Human Geography
Stockholm University

Introduction

In recent decades, Africa's urban population has been experiencing rapid growth, largely due to rural-urban migration. In 2009, almost 40 per cent of Africa's total population of one billion people was living in cities. The African urban population will grow further and is expected to triple over the next 40 years (UN-HABITAT 2010: 99). Africa includes megacities such as Cairo and Lagos that exceeded 10 million inhabitants by 2010, but 70 per cent of African urban population growth is expected to take place in small and medium-sized cities (UN-HABITAT 2010: 52–4).

Urban growth increases demand for housing and services in African cities and results in expansion of informal settlements. Although access to adequate and affordable housing is a recognised human right, enshrined in the Article 11, paragraph 1 of the International Covenant on Economic, Social and Cultural Rights (ICESCR), in 2010 nearly 200 million people in sub-Saharan Africa, or 62 per cent of the total urban population, were living in slums.[1] Slum dwellers live in conditions of deprivation and are vulnerable to forced eviction (UN-HABITAT 2008: 32–3). The African slum population is on a growing trend, as two-thirds of new urban inhabitants are expected to be housed in informal settlements (UN-HABITAT 2008: 33).[2] A large share of forced evictions takes place in Africa. Between 2003 and 2006, about two million of 5.5 million estimated evictions worldwide occurred on the African continent (COHRE 2006: 11). Evictions often take place without prior consultation, compensation or alternative habitation and involve violence. They can lead to loss of possessions and also of livelihoods (du Plessis 2005: 123–5).

Different strategies are being put forward to address urban poverty in general and the lack of access to adequate housing in particular. In this paper, I compare and contrast the arguments of two current discourses prominent in the development field and dealing with issues of urban poverty: 'Legal Empowerment of the Poor' and the 'Right to the City'. I particularly focus on the arguments they advance regarding access to housing in urban Africa.

These two discourses do not deal exclusively with the housing sector, but

---

1. For UN-HABITAT's slum criteria, see UN-HABITAT 2008: 33.
2. In this paper, I refer to informal settlements rather than slums, as I wish to emphasise their lack of legal recognition, which also varies between settlements and over time.

are also relevant to other social sectors. My choice to focus on housing in urban Africa stems from the significant challenges related to access to adequate housing in fast-growing African cities. The scope of those challenges requires a well-informed assessment of different housing policies, whether proposed or implemented. Thus, the purpose of the analysis is to gain an in-depth understanding of the arguments, normative and ideological background and major advocates of the respective discourses, thereby allowing for a well-informed assessment of their influence on ongoing or proposed housing policies.

While acknowledging that the two discourses are put forward by a variety of actors with sometimes differing views, in my analysis of their approaches towards the housing sector I focus on two particular types of sources that, I believe, most adequately reflect the African context. In the case of legal empowerment, I examine the report by the high-level CLEP, which represents the dominant view on legal empowerment. Although its recommendations are directed towards all developing countries, it includes many references to the African continent. Regarding the Right to the City, I consider a number of grassroots movements, NGOs and academics that invoke the Right to the City specifically in the African context. It must be noted that academic researchers documenting the struggles of social movements for the Right to the City tend to sympathise with the cause, which may influence their interpretations. However, in the absence of my own field research, I cannot avoid relying on those secondary sources.

Human geographer Loretta Lees (2004: 104) highlights two major components of analysis of urban discourse: (1) interpretative context, that is the social setting in which the discourse occurs and (2) the rhetorical organisation or argumentative schema that shapes a text or discourse and establishes its authority. In following this method, I look both at the arguments within the two discourses and also at the social and ideological context in which they were developed, as well as that of their major critics.

I begin by contrasting their respective theoretical backgrounds, major arguments and advocates, recognised limitations as well as their normative foundations. Bearing these elements in mind, I then compare their respective approaches to the issue of access to housing in the urban African context, focusing on their understanding of existing problems and their proposed solutions. I argue that these discourses have divergent approaches to access to housing, with legal empowerment emphasising the role of individual property rights and the Right to the City stressing collective and public services. These divergences in turn imply differences in terms of their policy recommendations, without necessarily implying that those recommendations are incompatible.

Part I:
'Legal Empowerment of the Poor' and 'Right to the City' discourses

1. Legal Empowerment of the Poor

Over the past two decades, the concept of 'empowerment' has become increasingly fashionable in the development field. It is commonly viewed as a process of giving voice to poor people and increasing their capacity to influence and make choices about their lives (Banik 2009: 127). The concept of empowerment, however, has a variety of meanings and interpretations (Eyben and Napier-Moore 2009). In this paper, I adopt Naila Kabeer's (2002: 3) view of empowerment as the 'expansion in people's ability to make strategic life choices in a context where this ability was previously denied to them'.

The concept of Legal Empowerment of the Poor is based on the recognition that rule of law reforms in developing countries seldom benefit the poor or bring development and democracy (Banik 2009: 128). As Golub (2003: 6-7) explains, in most developing countries, 'laws benefiting the poor exist on paper but not in practice unless the poor or their allies push for the laws' enforcement'. In contrast, the LEP concept seeks to expand the benefits of the rule of law for all citizens. It, therefore, implies the 'use of legal services and related development activities to increase disadvantaged populations' control over their lives' (Golub 2003: 25).

Theoretical background: de Soto's 'Mystery of Capital'

A central component of the LEP concept is property formalisation, which was brought to international attention from the mid-1980s by the Peruvian liberal economist Hernando de Soto, who advocates the granting of formal property rights to the poor as a strategy for addressing poverty in developing countries (1989; 2000; 2001). More recently, the LEP concept gained prominence in the UN arena with the establishment and work of CLEP between 2005 and 2008. The commission was hosted by UNDP and comprised eminent thinkers and decision-makers, such as former heads of state and ministers, and was co-chaired by de Soto and former US Secretary of State Madeleine Albright. It included individuals of varied background, such as former Mexican President Ernesto Zedillo, former American Treasury Secretary Lawrence Summers, Iranian human-rights activist and Nobel Prize winner Shirin Ebadi, as well as Allan Larsson, former finance minister of Sweden (CLEP 2008: v-vi).

Although efforts to formalise property have existed since governments first attempted to regulate the economy,[3] it is de Soto who has largely brought the issue into international debates. In *The Other Path* (1989) and *The Mystery of Capital* (2000), de Soto argues that poverty persists because poor people do not enjoy legal property rights. On the basis of his observations of the functioning of the informal economy in Peru and other developing countries, he explains that while most poor people in such countries possess land and businesses, they lack legal property rights to these assets and cannot thus use them as capital to create wealth, notably as guarantees to secure credit and infrastructure. For that reason, he considers that the assets of the poor are undervalued and qualify as 'dead capital' (de Soto 2001: 13–14, 17).

De Soto identifies two main obstacles to the formalisation of the assets of the poor. First, most property in the informal sector cannot be documented and informal proofs of ownership are not accepted in formal law. Second, even when ownership has been determined, the assets held in the informal sector need to be linked to contracts and legal instruments of modern market societies if they are to be used for productive purposes (de Soto 2001: 35–7). De Soto concludes that the continuation and stability of the market system largely requires that poor citizens in developing countries start enjoying the benefits of the market economy (de Soto 2001: 42).

De Soto's theory has received mixed responses. On one hand, his ideas were acclaimed by the World Bank and several governments across the world – including Egypt, Peru, El Salvador and Tanzania, which requested the help of de Soto's Lima-based foundation, the Institute for Liberty and Democracy (ILD) to implement formalisation programmes (ILD 2011). On the other, de Soto's argument faced much criticism from left-oriented academics, development practitioners and activists on the grounds that it was neoliberal in considering legal titling and market inclusion as the solution to poverty (Davis 2004: 25–7; Harvey 2008: 36–7). Critics also questioned the efficiency and practicability of his proposal (Gilbert 2002; Green 2008: 72–3; Payne *et al.* 2009: 453–5; Royston 2006: 170–6; Varley 2002).

For all these reasons, the appointment of de Soto as CLEP co-chair provoked significant discontent among civil society and academics. Yet the 'Making the Law Work for Everyone' report (hereafter the Report) produced by the commission (2008) moved beyond de Soto's liberal focus on property rights to adopt a broader view that legal empowerment as a global social contract

---

3. The term 'informal economy', however, is relatively recent, as it was first coined by the British anthropologist Keith Hart (1973), who referred to it in the context of the urban employment sector in Ghana.

involved a so-called 'bundle of rights', including labour rights and the right to access credit (Banik 2009: 118-19).

The Report is a key reference in current debates on legal empowerment and deserves close attention. The following sections outline its major arguments and the major critiques.

The CLEP Report: arguments in favour of Legal Empowerment

CLEP identified four central pillars of legal empowerment that are considered to be interdependent and mutually reinforcing: (1) access to justice and the rule of law, (2) property rights, (3) labour rights, and (4) 'business rights' (Banik 2009: 5). These pillars constituted the themes of CLEP's four working groups (Stephens 2009: 141).

The Report is based on the premise that 'four billion people around the world are robbed of the chance to better their lives and climb out of poverty, because they are excluded from the rule of law' (CLEP 2005: 1). The first pillar, access to justice and the rule of law, is therefore considered the 'fundamental and enabling framework' of the three remaining pillars. As concrete policy measures, the Report suggests, among others, ensuring the right to legal identity, creating accessible judicial and land administration systems that recognise and integrate customary and informal legal procedures, and focusing on the legal empowerment of specific groups such as women, refugees, indigenous populations and internally displaced persons (CLEP 2005: 5–6). It is worth underlining that the Report recommends that 'customary legal norms and structures are not abolished, but rather recognised and incorporated within a modern titling regime' (Stephens 2009: 148).

The second pillar – property rights – is based on the assumption that 'ownership of property, alone or in association with others, is a human right'. The Report therefore includes a set of recommendations for supporting poor people to 'use property as collateral for obtaining credit, such as business loan or mortgage' (CLEP 2005: 7). Although private property is the central focus of the Report, collective property is also promoted in cases where legal cultures recognise traditional community-based ownership of natural resources (CLEP 2005: 65). The two first pillars of the Report are in line with de Soto's original ideas as they emphasise the importance of access to the rule of law and legal property rights as a means for accessing credit and creating capital.

The third pillar of the Report focusing on labour rights proposes the following measures: creation of employment opportunities; improvement of the regulation and functioning of labour markets; effectively enforcing social protection mechanisms (medical care, health insurance, pensions and the like) to protect against shocks; implementing a core sets of workers' rights in the informal sector; promoting gender equality and fulfilling national obligations to meet ILO standards (CLEP 2005: 8). The inclusion of labour rights in the Report adds an important social component to the LEP approach and is a clear departure from de Soto's narrow focus on individual property rights.

Finally, the fourth pillar, business rights, refers to the ability of the poor to access basic financial services as well as 'protections and opportunities such as the ability to contract, to make deals, to raise investment capital through shares, bonds, or other means, and to pass ownership from one generation to another' (CLEP 2005: 9). Although de Soto does not refer to 'business rights' *per se*, this concept is in line with his argument that property formalisation will enhance the ability of the poor to access credit and other financial services and that excessive bureaucratic hurdles are major obstacles to the development of businesses by them.

The Report argues that LEP is a motor for systemic and progressive change in society. First, the formalisation of informal assets allows for increased tax revenues, which could be used to promote national development. Economic gains also expand local markets and increase economic activity. Second, the spread of the rule of law prevents 'predatory networks' from exploiting vulnerable individuals in the informal sector, leading to reductions in crime and unrest. Finally, it argues that such transformation can increase government credibility among previously marginalised individuals (CLEP 2005: 5–6).

Critiques of the CLEP Report

Although the Report was praised for bringing the LEP concept to the forefront of international debate, it prompted a number of criticisms among academics and practitioners on both conceptual and operational grounds (Banik 2008; Faundez 2009; Payne *et al.* 2009; Stephens 2009). Interestingly, the critical reviews of the Report come predominantly from Western left-oriented social scientists and development practitioners.

From a conceptual perspective, Dan Banik[4] (2009: 119) is critical of the

4. Dan Banik, associate professor of political science at the Centre for Development and the Environment, University of Oslo, has done extensive research on legal empowerment. He is the head of the Academic Network on Legal Empowerment of the Poor (ANLEP), established in 2007 to undertake research and disseminate research findings on selected topics that have been crucial to the work of CLEP (ANLEP 2011).

Report's assumption that it is the lack of secure and protected assets and work that keep individuals in poverty. In making that claim, the Report ignores the wide range of other important factors that cause and perpetuate poverty. These include low economic growth, social exclusion, inadequate social services, high population growth, environmental degradation, social and political instability, vulnerability to debt, disease and natural disaster. By focusing exclusively on the formalisation and protection of the assets of the poor, the Report disregards the findings of a large body of literature on poverty and development. Banik therefore regrets the lack of clarity regarding the basis on which the four LEP pillars were identified and wonders how the LEP approach relates to other legal issues relevant to poverty reduction, such as education, violence against women, inequality and social exclusion (Banik 2009: 125). Banik also notes that the conceptual link between the LEP approach and human rights principles is not explicitly described, which further undermines its conceptual foundation (Banik 2009: 122).

From an operational perspective, many commentators, even though they may endorse the goal of LEP, regret that the Report does not pay sufficient attention to the numerous operational and political challenges facing its implementation (Banik 2009; Faundez 2009; Payne *et al.* 2009; Stephens 2009).

One set of critiques relates to the potential of asset formalisation to exclude marginalised groups and concomitantly favour more powerful ones. Such effects could occur where customary law[5] treats certain groups (such as women) inequitably (Faundez 2009: 2; Joireman 2008: 1235–41; Stephens 2009: 148). The Report calls for the integration of customary and informal legal procedures used by the poor into the formal judicial system (CLEP 2008: 5). Yet several studies attest that customary law is sometimes used as an instrument by certain groups, such as traditional leaders, to assert power over less powerful groups (Joireman 2008: 1235–37).[6] Property formalisation can be detrimental to women where they enjoy weaker property and inheritance rights than men (Joireman 2008: 1239). It follows that any attempt to implement LEP would require the definition and enforcement of 'good and inclusive' laws (Faundez 2009: 11; Stephens 2009: 134).

---

5. Since colonial times, customary law has been used by various ethnic groups in sub-Saharan Africa to regulate their internal affairs, including land ownership, marriage and inheritance. Customary law is recognised by courts in sub-Saharan Africa as a body of law secondary to statutory law (Joireman 2008: 1235).

6. For examples of customary law being used as an instrument by certain groups to assert power over others, see Joireman (2009).

In addition, studies show that people living in poverty sometimes distrust legal institutions and choose to remain in the informal realm. First, titling often involves high costs which can discourage people from seeking to formalise their assets (Gilbert 2002: 8–9; Varley 2002: 457). Second, granting property rights to the poor does not guarantee that such rights will be enforced by courts and local administrations, which may lack resources or be corrupt (Joireman 2008: 1241).

The idea that asset formalisation will automatically lead to access to credit is also contested. Evidence shows that financing institutions are reluctant to lend to the poor regardless of their formal titles, while the poor may fear to use their titles as guarantees to obtain loans. It is also often the case that poor people receiving formal property titles sell them and return to the informal market (Gilbert 2002: 14–18; Green 2008: 72–3; Payne *et al.* 2009: 453–5; Royston 2006: 170–6; Varley 2002: 455–8).

Another critique of the Report relates to its lack of emphasis on the political obstacles in the way of the legal empowerment agenda. Reforms in this area are likely to face resistance from a variety of actors, such as political leaders, economic elites, rural landholders or civil society, who may fear for their privileges. Hence, the success of LEP depends heavily on the reformers' ability to address opposition (Stephens 2009: 148–9, 152; Banik 2009: 130). In addition, many of the Report's policy recommendations, such as labour rights, involve significant costs. Consequently, policy-makers in developing countries may lack the political will or resources to engage in reform. In that respect, Stephens regrets that the Report does not provide sufficient empirical evidence of successful legal empowerment projects that would justify investment in similar projects rather than in other development strategies. He also criticises the Report for its lack of guidance regarding the prioritisation and phasing of its policy recommendations (Stephens 2009: 134–5, 152).

A final critique highlights the fact that, although the Report presents the LEP as a bottom-up development strategy, since it calls for the participation of people living in poverty in the design and implementation of its policies and ownership of those policies (CLEP 2008: 77), it offers top-down and state-centred recommendations (Banik 2009: 129; Stephens 2009: 133).

Normative foundations of the CLEP Report

To provide a better understanding of the ideological and conceptual basis of the CLEP's approach to legal empowerment, this section analyses its normative foundations. In particular, it examines the types of rights that underpin it and argues that the emphasis is on civil and political rights and to a lesser extent on social and economic rights. In that sense, LEP can be seen as inspired by classical liberal ideas.

Human rights are commonly classified into three distinct generations: (1) civil and political rights, designed to protect the liberty, security and physical and spiritual integrity of the human person; (2) economic, social and cultural rights, including the right to just and favourable conditions of work, social security, adequate food, clothing, housing and health; and finally (3) collective rights, such as rights to self-determination. Each of these generations of rights also involves a specific role for the state. The state is expected to guarantee civil and political rights, finance and actively promote economic, social and cultural rights and respect collective rights (Green 2008: 25; Van Boven 1979: 48).

The pillars of LEP put forward in the Report encompass a mix of civil, political and social and economic rights. The first, second and fourth pillars, dealing with access to justice and the rule of law and property rights and business rights, represent civil and political rights. The rule of law and property rights are classical liberal ideas that emerged in the 17th and 18th centuries with the aim of limiting the power of the state. The rule of law refers to the equality before the law of each individual, including state officials, and is the core principle of civil and political rights. The modern concept of property rights was first developed by John Locke, who argued that individuals have a natural right to life, liberty and property (Jones 1994: 75–6). Locke's conception of property rights is in line with the legal empowerment approach, which advocates the right of all individuals to enjoy legal protection of their private property. However, the Report also allows for the recognition of collective property in contexts where community-based ownership of natural resources is well-functioning and part of local tradition (CLEP 2008: 65). 'Business rights' could, at first sight, be considered second generation economic rights, as they could suggest an active role by the state in promoting business activity. However, they are actually an extension of property rights as they do not involve a redistributive role for the state but instead focus on liberalisation and the removal of bureaucratic hurdles to business.

By contrast, the third pillar, labour rights, represents second generation social and economic rights entailing active state involvement in their implementation. The coexistence of different types of rights in the Report is partly explained by its broad agenda and the diversity of understandings of legal empowerment among the CLEP members. During the negotiations and drafting of the Report, CLEP was divided into working groups, each focusing on a particular pillar. It is argued that this led to 'dislocation of efforts' and that

17

conceptual consensus was probably never reached among commission members (Stephens 2009: 141).

Despite the presence of labour rights and recognition of collective property rights, the emphasis of the Report is on individual civil and political rights, as most of the pillars relate to those rights, and access to justice and rule of law is presented as the 'fundamental and enabling framework' of the three remaining pillars (CLEP 2008: 31).

More generally, emphasis on first generation individual rights is a recurrent trend in today's society. At times of market liberalisation and state withdrawal, civil and political rights are gaining more prominence over economic, social, cultural and collective rights (Hirschl 2000: 1096).[7] Nevertheless, the Right to the City discourse, the focus of the next section, adopts a different approach, emphasising second and third generation rights.

---

7. Hirschl (2000: 1095) also notes that economic and social rights have received few if any positive court rulings in comparison with civil and political rights. He explains this trend on the grounds that social and economic rights are a threat to human liberty and equality. The conflict opposing civil and political rights to economic, social and cultural rights is also reflected in the formulation of two separate covenants: the International Covenant on Civil and Political Rights (1966) and the International Covenant on Economic, Social and Cultural Rights (1976) (Van Boven 1979).

2. The Right to the City

Theoretical background: Lefebvre's Right to the City

While the LEP concept is grounded in classical liberal ideas, the Right to the City notion emerged out of a Marxist-inspired philosophical tradition. It was first coined by the French philosopher and sociologist Henri Lefebvre in 1968 in *Le Droit à la ville* (Lefebvre 1996: 158–9). Today, the notion has been rehabilitated and reinterpreted by social movements, academics and international agencies, notably UN-HABITAT and UNESCO (Costes 2010: 181).

Written in the context of the sociopolitical student movements of May 1968 in Paris, *Le Droit à la ville* describes processes of major political and economic restructuring undergone by cities in Europe and beyond as a result of the expansion of the capitalist mode of production. Lefebvre argues that the industrial city is being replaced by a new urban phenomenon characterised by the bursting of the city into peripheries and suburbs and the gentrification of urban centres. In this new urban landscape driven by the logic of profitability, functionality requirements take precedence over social aspects. Spaces of segregation emerge confining inhabitants to particular zones according to their social group, age or ethnic background – such as working class and immigrants in 'ghettos', students in 'campuses' and privileged groups in 'residential areas' (Costes 2010: 180). According to Lefebvre, these new processes have led urban inhabitants to lose control over the decisions that shape the city (Purcell 2002: 99).

As an alternative to this 'neoliberal disenfranchisement' and decline in democracy in 'post-industrial' cities, Lefebvre proposes a political programme of urban reform whereby urban inhabitants would reappropriate the urban space and claim their 'Right to the City'. Lefebvre's Right to the City entails a radical restructuring of social, political and economic relations in the city and beyond that would shift control away from the capital and the state towards urban inhabitants with the aim of furthering 'the interests of the whole society and firstly of all those who *inhabit*' (Lefebvre 1996: 158). The Right to the City involves the inhabitants' increased influence not only in relation to the state but also to the economic sphere – including firms (Purcell 2002: 102). Lefebvre also considers that the Right to the City should be enjoyed by all urban inhabitants ('citadins') or those who *inhabit the city*, regardless of their nationality. In that sense, his theory is a radical questioning of the liberal-democratic notion of citizenship based on the nation state as a framework for determining eligibility for rights (Purcell 2002: 102).

Lefebvre's Right to the City encompasses two different rights for urban inhabitants: the right to participation and the right to appropriation. The first contends that any decision affecting the city should involve urban inhabitants. The right to appropriation implies the right of urban inhabitants to physically access and use urban space. In Lefebvre's words, the Right to the City is a right to 'renewed centrality, to places of encounter and exchange, to life rhythms and time uses, enabling the full and complete *usage* of these moments and places' (Lefebvre 1996: 179). However, the right to appropriation is not only the right to access urban space, but also to 'produce' it in order to meet the needs of urban inhabitants. As human geographer David Harvey (2008: 23) puts it, 'the right to the city is far more than the individual liberty to access urban resources: it is a right to change ourselves by changing the city.' Urban space is thus not conceived as private property but rather as being collectively owned by the city's inhabitants.

Major advocates of the Right to the City and their arguments

Lefebvre's concept of the Right of the City has seen a revival in recent years as an alternative to urbanisation based on neoliberal policies. This revival took place in the context of increased recognition of the social exclusion and inequalities generated by neoliberal policies around the world, notably privatisation and state withdrawal. A variety of actors, including left-oriented academics,[8] grassroots social movements, NGOs, governmental bodies and international development agencies, have reinterpreted Lefebvre's concept and used it in different ways (Costes 2010: 189).

Two main approaches can be distinguished among the current advocates of the Right to the City. On one hand, there is a radical strand whose views have remained close to Lefebvre's initial concept and who consider the Right to the City as a moral claim or oppositional demand rather than as a legal instrument (Mayer 2009: 367). From this perspective, the Right to the City is a political tool to mobilise broad social sectors around the struggle for social justice in the city. This approach includes grassroots social movements, such as City Alliance in the US, and left-oriented academics (Mayer 2009: 367). The Marxist geographer David Harvey (2008: 39–40), for example, views the

---

8. Notable academics engaging with the Right to the City include John Friedmann (1995), Saskia Sassen (1996), Edward Soja (1991) and David Harvey (2008).

Right to the City as a means to unify the struggles against processes of social exclusion generated in the context of urbanisation under capitalism.

On the other hand, a more 'depoliticised' or 'reformist' approach to the Right to the City, advanced by certain civil society movements, NGOs, municipalities and international development agencies, favours 'institutionalisation' of the Right to the City: that is, its official recognition as a new collective right in international, regional and national human rights documents. In recent years, a number of declarations and legislative documents on the Right to the City have been developed worldwide, and aim to influence urban policy and legislation towards greater social justice and equity (Mayer 2009: 367–8).[9]

The most notable example is the World Charter on the Right to the City. This emerged within the framework of the World Social Forum, led by Latin American civil society movements, and the Habitat International Coalition, a non-profit alliance of organisations working on human settlements. The formulation and negotiation of the Charter started at the first World Social Forum in 2001 and was completed at the World Social Forum in Porto Alegre in 2005 (Ortiz 2010: 117).

The World Charter on the Right to the City is intended to serve as a legal instrument that is both universal and compact so that it can be adopted by the UN system, regional human rights systems and governments as a new collective human right (Ortiz 2010: 117).

The Charter defines the Right to the City as:

> … the equitable usufruct of cities within the principles of sustainability, democracy, equity, and social justice. It is the collective right of the inhabitants of cities, in particular of the vulnerable and marginalised groups, that confers upon them legitimacy of action and organisation, based on their uses and customs, with the objective to achieve full exercise of the right to free self-determination and an adequate standard of living. (World Charter on the Right to the City 2005, Article I)

The Charter proposes three major dimensions for the Right to the City: (1) the full exercise of citizenship by realising all human rights to ensure collective well-being; (2) the democratic management of the city through citizen participation, either direct or indirect, in the definition and implementation of all public policies affecting the city; (3) the social function of the city through

9. Examples of instruments and tools inspired by the concept of the Right to the City can be found in the UNESCO and UN-HABITAT report 'Urban Policies and the Right to the City: Rights, responsibilities and citizenship' (Brown and Kristiansen 2009).

the prioritisation of projects and investments that benefit the community as a whole and meet criteria of distributive equity and environmental sustainability (World Charter on the Right to the City 2005, Article II).

While Lefebvre viewed the Right to the City as independent of any institutionalised right, the World Charter presents it as encompassing a collection of already recognised human rights. These include civil and political rights, such as the right to public information and political participation, and economic, social and cultural rights, such as the right to work in equitable and satisfactory conditions; social security; the right to water, food, housing; the right to health, education and culture; and respect for diversity and ethnic, racial, sexual and cultural plurality (World Charter on the Right to the City 2005, Part II and III). From this perspective, it could be argued that the World Charter does not demand radical transformation of existing urban governance, but rather the better enforcement of existing human rights (Mayer 2009: 369).

In parallel with civil society and NGO-led initiatives such as the World Charter, a number of charters and legal documents have been initiated by government bodies and local municipalities. Among others, there is the European Charter to Safeguard Human Rights in the City (Saint-Denis, France, 2000 and endorsed by a number of European cities); the City Statute of Brazil (2001); and the Montreal Charter of Rights and Responsibilities (Canada, 2006) (Ortiz 2010: 114).

UN agencies have also promoted the concept of the Right to the City. In 2005, UNESCO and UN-HABITAT jointly launched a project on urban policies and the Right to the City by seeking to build alliances among local authorities and others on public policy and legislation that promotes development, local democracy, social equity and justice. The UN-HABITAT also chose the Right to the City as the central theme of the fifth World Urban Forum held in Rio de Janeiro in 2010 (UNESCO, UN-HABITAT 2009: 11).

Criticism of the Right to the City discourse

Several critiques have emerged focusing both on the conceptual foundations of the Right to the City and its current reinterpretations and uses. In this section, I discuss two major critiques: first, a conceptual critique related to the focus on the city (or on the local scale) (Purcell 2002, 2006); and second a critique of the loss of radicalism in current accounts of the Right to the City (Lopes de Souza 2010; Mayer 2009, Unger 2009).

A major challenge for the concept of the Right to the City lies in the difficulty of defining the 'city' and 'urban inhabitants'. What are the limits of the city? Who can be considered an urban inhabitant? In liberal democracies, individuals are entitled to certain rights on the basis of a liberal-democratic conception of citizenship within the framework of the nation state. The concept of the Right to the City, however, questions this conception and claims that individuals and groups are entitled to the Right to the City as inhabitants of a city rather than as citizens of a nation state. In that sense, the Right to the City privileges the urban scale over other scales of political community (Purcell 2002: 105).

Yet the American geographer Mark Purcell, who has extensively analysed Lefebvre's Right to the City, argues that scales defining political membership – such as the urban scale – 'are not pre-given or self-evident, but rather they are socially produced through political struggle' (Purcell 2002: 105). It follows that determining who is entitled to the Right to the City and who is not will have to be defined through a process of political struggle. Conflicts regarding eligibility for the Right to the City could emerge where a political decision made in the city impacts individuals beyond the city. Conflicts could also occur when a political decision would affect certain inhabitants of the city more than others (Purcell 2002: 104).

Based on the claim that scales of political membership are socially constructed, Purcell also questions the focus on the urban scale as the most appropriate for political participation. He warns that the Right to the City risks falling into the 'local trap' or the assumption that the local scale is inherently more democratic than others (Purcell 2006: 1921).

The question of the focus on the city and of leaving aside rural areas was widely debated in the negotiation of the World Charter. It was particularly raised by individuals from Asian and African countries, who argued that the Right to the City primarily reflected Euro-American realities and neglected the priorities and challenges of other parts of the world. In African and Asian contexts, 'city' sometimes has an 'exclusionary' connotation. In Asia, for example, the city often refers to the formal territorial space where middle and upper classes live and evokes rejection of popular settlements and evictions (Ortiz 2010: 119). In addition, as the majority of the population in Asia and Africa live in rural areas, some peasant movements such as Via Campesina[10] argue that the Right to the City diverts attention from the social problems faced by rural communities. A debate is taking place among advocates of the

---

10. Via Campesina is an international movement comprising peasants, landless people, women farmers, indigenous people, migrants and agricultural workers from around the world.

Right to the City and rural movements with the objective of articulating a common strategy without denying the specifics of each context (Ortiz 2010: 120).[11]

The second major critique relates to the perceived loss of radicalism in current approaches to the Right to the City in comparison with Lefebvre's original concept. As already mentioned, the Right to the City is advocated by a variety of actors with different opinions and strategies. While Lefebvre conceived the Right to the City as a political tool for the radical transformation of capitalist urban society, some of its current proponents see it as a legal tool and demand its institutionalisation in existing human rights documents. This approach has led some left-oriented academics and civil society activists to argue that the original Right to the City as a transformative movement has been diluted (Lopes de Souza 2010: 315–16; Mayer 2009: 369–70). Brazilian left-libertarian urbanist Marcelo Lopes de Souza (2010: 315–16) argues that, given the heterogeneity of the actors advocating the Right to the City – including social movements from both North and the South, local governments, UN agencies and NGOs – the concept has become an 'umbrella phrase' encompassing claims for affordable housing, democratic participation and environmental sustainability. From that perspective, the Right to the City has become a banner or a rallying cry for struggles against the harmful effects of neoliberalism. Yet some critics argue that these struggles amount to a demand for a 'more gentle neoliberalism' rather than contestation (Mayer 2009: 366, 370).

Not only is the content of the Right to the City considered to have changed, but also the type of the actors promoting it. German political scientist Margit Mayer observes a professionalisation and bureaucratisation within Right to the City campaigns. The struggles of grassroots activists and deprived urban groups seem to have been overshadowed by development institutions and international NGOs. In the words of Knut Unger (2009), an activist in a German tenant organisation, some Right to the City documents reflect 'a top down agenda agreed on by some NGOs networks who already know what the rights are, but want to build a larger alliance for improved power for which they need a name and branding'.

---

11. It must be noted that the World Charter on the Right to the City (2005) refers to the city as including 'the urban space as well as the rural or semi-rural surroundings that form part of its territory' (World Charter on the Right to the City 2005, Article I).

Normative foundations of the Right to the City

I have previously argued that the concept of legal empowerment is inspired by liberal ideas that emphasise individual civil and political rights, notably the right to private property. In this section, I show that the concept of the Right to the City is influenced by Marxist ideology and that its current more 'reformist' versions reflect socio-democratic principles conferring a strong role on the state in welfare provision. However, the Right to the City differs from socio-democratic principles in its conception of citizenship.

While the LEP concept is grounded in the liberal principle of private property rights, the concept of the Right to the City was conceived as a challenge to the capitalist model of development based on the primacy of capital accumulation and private property. Influenced by Marxist theory, Lefebvre developed the Right to the City in response to urbanisation under capitalism, which led to increased social exclusion and a decline in democracy in 'post-industrial' cities. In his view, the struggle for the Right to the City is essentially a class conflict (Harvey 2008: 28).

Contrary to the LEP, which emphasises legal rights and the rule of law for the welfare of citizens, Lefebvre considered the Right to the City as a political tool. A second major difference with the legal empowerment approach relates to the conception of citizenship. While LEP abides by the liberal-democratic conception of political citizenship within the framework of the nation state, the Right to the City aims at empowering *all urban inhabitants* and not simply *national citizens* (Purcell 2002: 102). Moreover, Lefebvre's Right to the City is a collective, third generation, right enjoyed by urban inhabitants, in contrast with the predominantly individual rights put forward by LEP (Parnell and Pieterse 2010: 149).

As noted earlier, Lefebvre's Right to the City encompasses two main rights for urban inhabitants – to participation and to appropriation – which are significantly different from the rights put forward by LEP.

First, the right to participation demands that urban inhabitants be involved in any decision affecting the city. It shifts control from the capital and state elites towards the inhabitants, who are considered the majority and hegemonic voice (Purcell 2002: 103). LEP also promotes increased political participation by people living in poverty in the decisions affecting them. The CLEP Report (2008: 9, 68) calls for a bottom-up approach to ensure civil society participation in defining and implementing legal empowerment projects. However, as already noted the Report's recommendations are predominantly top-down and state-centred (Banik 2009: 129; Stephens 2009: 133).

In addition, the emphasis seems to be on economic, rather than political, participation (CLEP 2008: 18, 22, 81).

Second, the right to appropriation implies the right of urban inhabitants to use urban space and change it in order to meet their needs. It differs from the right to property in considering the city as collectively owned by urban inhabitants, in sharp contrast with the concept of private and, mostly, individual ownership put forward by LEP (Harvey 2008: 23; Purcell 2002: 103). The World Charter on the Right to the City (2005) also emphasises the 'social function' as a primary purpose of the city: that is, to guarantee 'for all its inhabitants full usufruct of the resources offered by the city'. Paragraph 2.4 states the primacy of collective interest: 'In the formulation and implementation of urban policies, the collective social and cultural interest should prevail above individual property rights and speculative interests.'

The recent 'reformist' advocates of the Right to the City use the concept as a banner in their struggles for social inclusion and respect for the human rights of poor and marginalised people. The World Charter on the Right to the City, for example, promotes recognised human rights, as well as some new rights, to ensure adequate standards of living for all urban inhabitants. Although the Charter includes both first and second generation rights, the focus is clearly on the latter. Emphasising the social function of the city, the Charter encompasses most economic, social and cultural rights, such as the right to social services, adequate housing and culture. This implies a strong role for the state as provider of well-being for urban inhabitants. Thus, many current advocates of the concept promote socio-democratic principles. The Right to the City therefore contrasts with the legal empowerment approach, which belongs to the liberal tradition favouring limited state intervention and mainly promoting first generation civil and political rights.

Part II:
Case study

3. Legal Empowerment of the Poor and Right to the City approaches towards housing in the urban African context

Having explored the LEP and Right to the City discourses, I now compare their approaches to the issue of housing in urban Africa. I first look at their respective understandings of the problems in the housing sector in Africa and then examine their proposed solutions. I use the CLEP Report (2008) as the basis of the LEP approach and, to reflect the perspectives of the Right to the City, I refer to a number of African grassroots movements such as AbM and the Western Cape Anti-Eviction Campaign (South Africa), international NGOs such as the global alliance SDI, which is active in South Africa and Ghana and elsewhere (Afenah 2010; Bradlow 2010), and the Centre on Housing Rights and Evictions (COHRE) (COHRE 2006; du Plessis 2005). The actions of these grassroots movements are well documented and discussed by 'supportive' academics on whose research I largely base my analysis (Huchzermeyer 2010; Miraftab 2009; Parnell and Pieterse 2010; Pithouse 2010). I chose these particular actors because their advocacy of the Right to the City specifically relates to African cities. For the same reason, I decided not to consider the World Charter on the Right to the City, which aims at universal application. In addition, I found few initiatives by African municipalities related to the Right to the City, unlike in other regions.[12]

It must be noted that the actors promoting the Right to the City in Africa have various characteristics, approaches and strategies. They range from grassroots movements with limited financing, such as AbM, to international NGOs with professional staff, such as SDI. They also differ in their preferred stance towards state actors, with some, including AbM and the Western Cape Anti-Eviction Campaign, favouring independence from the state and others, like SDI, encouraging partnership with the state and rejecting direct confrontation (Bradlow 2010: 48; Pithouse 2010: 49–53).[13] The differences among

---

12. One relevant African local authority initiative is the 'Civic and Citizens Pact' in Dakar (Senegal), endorsed in 2003, which sets out reciprocal responsibilities – the city has agreed to respect the diverse culture and beliefs of inhabitants, while community-based organisations have agreed to act in a socially responsible way (Brown and Kristiansen 2009: 45).

13. For a comparison of the nature and strategies of AbM and SDI in Durban, South Africa, see Pithouse 2010.

urban African advocates of the Right to the City mirrors the global divide between radical and more reformist advocates of the concept discussed earlier. Therefore, I attempt to highlight the common features of their arguments, while acknowledging the diversity in their nature and methods. Finally, one cannot but notice that much of the literature on the Right to the City in Africa focuses on South Africa (de Bruin 2010; Huchzermeyer 2009; Miraftab 2009; Parnell and Pieterse 2010; Pithouse 2010). This implies that the concept has not been evenly adopted across the continent. This in turn is related to the fact that the Right to the City is an 'imported' concept, having first been advocated by European and Latin-American civil society before spreading to other regions, particularly through the World Social Forum. South Africa's predominance in the literature could also be explained by its particular history and also possibly by the fact that South-African social movements have a more prominent place in academic research.

Identified problems regarding the housing sector in urban Africa

As the underlying cause of poor access to adequate housing, LEP discourse points to the absence of formal rights to land and property, whereas the Right to the City highlights the role of global economic, social and political processes.

In the LEP perspective, informality is at the root of housing problems for a number of reasons. First, the lack of formal title to prove ownership leaves informal settlement dwellers vulnerable to forced evictions, demolitions and bribery at the hands of public authorities (CLEP 2008: 33). Second, it constitutes a barrier to transferring or inheriting property, thereby exposing people to potential abuse in the illegal housing market (CLEP 2008: 35). Third, insecurity of tenure is also considered a cause of the poor quality of housing. From that perspective, lack of secure property titles can act as a disincentive to investing in maintenance and renovation (CLEP 2008: 50). Finally, insecurity of tenure is also viewed as a cause of poverty more generally, as property titles enable individuals to use their house as collateral in obtaining credit and making productive investments in their future (CLEP 2008: 49–51).

By contrast, advocates of the Right to the City underline several global trends in current urban governance policies that prevent most urban dwellers from accessing adequate and affordable housing and expose them to forced evictions. They argue that neoliberal urban policies, notably land market liberalisation and privatisation, produce growing social fragmentation in African cities between areas of prosperity and of marginality. Such policies, first introduced in African countries in the 1980s as part of the IMF's Structural Adjustment Programmes, lead to increased competition for valuable and well-located land in which the interests of affluent and powerful groups tend to prevail over those of poor communities (Fumtim 2010: 196–7; Huchzermeyer 2010: 25–6;). These policies reflect the governments' desire to turn African cities into globally competitive cities. For that purpose, they tend to prioritise investments in 'world class' infrastructure that is expected to attract foreign investors, international corporations, highly qualified professionals and tourists. Inevitably, such investments divert significant resources from investment in the social sector, such as low-cost quality housing construction or housing upgrading (Fumtim 2010: 197–8; Huchzermeyer 2010: 25–6; Miraftab 2009: 33; Pithouse 2010: 48). These efforts to increase urban competitiveness materialise through 'urban renewal' or 'beautification' initiatives involving the demolition of informal settlements and the removal of informal street trade. Forced evictions are sometimes accompanied by the relocation of inhabitants to peripheral areas, often situated far from where they pursue their livelihood activities (Huchzermeyer 2010: 28; du Plessis 2005; de Bruijn 2010). Large-scale evictions and relocations are particularly likely in the context of large international events such as global conferences or sports tournaments. The hosting of the FIFA World Cup in South Africa in June 2010, for example, was accompanied by large-scale evictions that triggered significant protest among informal settlement dwellers and street traders and led to a 'World Class Cities for All' campaign calling for the inclusion of poorer groups in the preparations for the event (Lindell *et al.* 2010; Fajemirokun 2010: 126–7; du Plessis 2005: 123). The Western Cape branch of AbM launched a 'Right to the City campaign' in May 2010 to show the world 'that this [South African] government is not accountable to the poor but to the rich' (de Bruijn 2010). From the protesters' perspective, urban governance tends to favour the interests of international investors and the economic and political elite, while excluding the majority of the population from the decisions directly affecting them.

In addition, African state officials tend to 'depoliticise' access to housing and present it as a technical rather than a political issue. In the case of South Africa, Pithouse (2010: 49) relates how government officials view housing as an issue requiring management and 'service delivery' from above, and disregard processes of community ownership. This lack of democratic participation in urban policies is seen as a denial of the Right to the City (Huchzermeyer 2010: 28; Pithouse 2010: 50).

The current situation in African cities is very different from the political and social context in which Lefebvre developed the Right to the City. Yet the processes of urban fragmentation, social segmentation and democratic deficit denounced by African activists are strongly reminiscent of the situation Lefebvre sought to address.

Proposed solutions for the housing sector in urban Africa

Given their different understandings of the problems of the housing sector in urban Africa, the LEP and Right to the City discourses also propose different solutions, the former focusing on formalisation of illegal housing and the latter on the right to housing irrespective of legal status and on participatory urban governance.

To enhance the access to urban land and adequate housing, the LEP approach calls for legal recognition of informal settlements (CLEP 2008: 35). To secure the property rights of informal settlement dwellers, it suggests a range of measures, including financial mechanisms, granting them adequate documentation for their already occupied lands or providing them with suitable alternatives, limiting administrative controls and establishing 'more robust and transparent guarantees in rental arrangements' (CLEP 2008: 65, 72). As noted above, the Report promotes not only individual ownership but also common property. In that respect, it recommends the establishment of 'legal frameworks enabling housing and land associations, allowing individual and common property to be combined by people with limited assets' (CLEP 2008: 65).

From the LEP perspective, providing access to home ownership is one of the key social policies states should implement to reinforce property rights. States can play a crucial role in enhancing house ownership by offering low interest loans and distributing state land. This, in turn, would boost the local economy through the housing sector and develop a skilled labour force (CLEP 2008: 68). It would also enable house owners to increase the productivity of their property by using it as collateral in obtaining credit, such as business loans or mortgages (CLEP 2008: 50). Finally, it is expected that house ownership will encourage owners to invest in home renovations, thereby increasing housing quality (CLEP 2008: 50).[14] The above suggests that, from the LEP perspective, governments can provide an initial impulse to pro-

14. The CLEP Report (2008: 50) cites two cases where provision of secure property rights led to improved housing conditions. In a shantytown in Argentina, it contributed to a 40 per cent increase in the number of houses with good quality walls and to a 47 per cent increase in those with quality roofs. In Lima, it boosted spending on housing renovation by 68 per cent.

mote private property in the housing sector and thereby spur a market-driven strategy for poverty alleviation.

With regard to evictions, the LEP approach condemns arbitrary evictions but considers evictions possible 'only in circumstances where physical safety of life and property is threatened, where contract agreements have not been fulfilled' and when they are executed in accordance with due process and compensation (CLEP 2008: 49). In other words, formalisation of house ownership is viewed as a safeguard against arbitrary eviction.

By contrast, Right to the City advocates do not view property formalisation as a solution to poor access to housing, but instead call for access to land and housing for all urban residents, regardless of the tenure status. They condemn forced evictions and any form of criminalisation of informal settlement dwellers. Instead, they strive for recognition of informal settlement as 'the best available housing option for millions of people despite its obvious imperfections' (Afenah 2010: 165; Fajemirokun 2010: 126; Pithouse 2010: 50; Parnell and Pieterse 2010: 153).

To that end, a growing number of African social movements and NGOs invoke the Right to the City characterised by the right to appropriation and participation. It is important to stress that the Right to the City is not same as the right to housing. Even though the Right to the City is much broader, its current advocates consider housing as a major component of the Right to the City.[15]

In the spirit of the right to appropriation, urban residents should have access to affordable and well-located shelter and basic services, which is a prerequisite for securing their livelihoods and well-being (Miraftab 2009: 36). Describing the AbM movement in Durban, Mathivet and Buckingham (2009) argue that 'these shack dwellers need not only a roof over their heads, but the right to remain where they are living in the city because with this right comes the ability to fulfill their rights to work, education, and healthcare.' Joseph Fumtim (2010: 195), Cameroonian coordinator of the Inter-African network of Inhabitants (RIAH), even equates the Right to the City with the right to life, as '[i]t aims to ensure that every citizen is able to exercise their basic biological functions with the utmost dignity'. Therefore, the right to appropriation supposes that the social value of the city is prioritised over its

---

15. The right to housing is one of the rights encompassed in the World Charter on the Right to the City (2005). Moreover, in the African context, much advocacy about the right to the city is related to access to housing and to countering forced evictions.

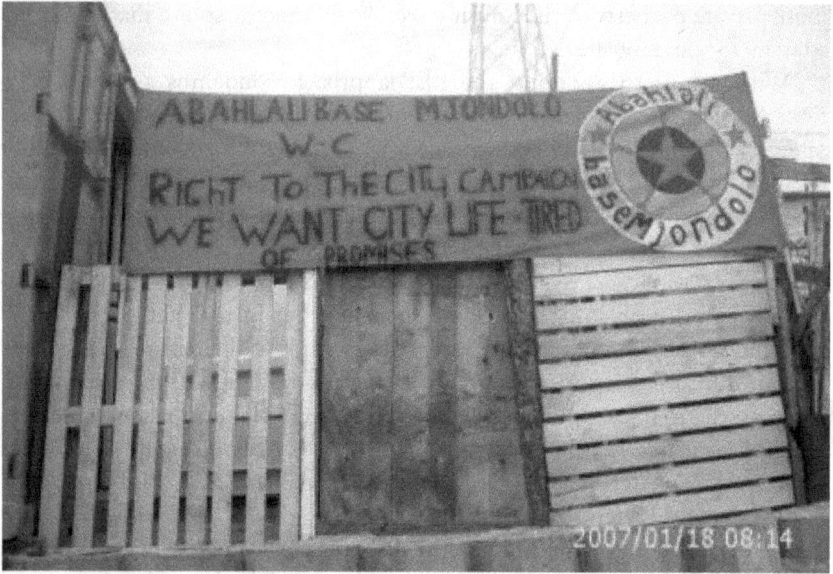

Picture from *The right to the city campaign*.
Abahlali baseMjondolo (http://abahlali.org/node/6750)

commercial value. It means reversing the social exclusion and urban fragmentation processes generated by the initiatives to achieve competitiveness and
'world class' standards (Huchzermeyer 2010: 28).

The right to participation implies more democratic and inclusive governance of the city. Regarding housing in particular, it presumes a move away
from a technocratic logic of delivery wherein informal settlement dwellers are
merely 'passive beneficiaries waiting for help' (Pithouse 2010: 53). The Right
to the City approach calls for participatory practices that allow for active
involvement of poorer inhabitants in the planning and implementation of
urban policies such as informal settlement 'upgrades'.[16]

---

16. The American urban planner Faranak Miraftab (2009: 40), however, warns that,
    in the current neoliberal era, the possibility of political inclusion does not gua-
    rantee substantive inclusion, that is, an improvement in livelihood situations. In
    post-apartheid South-Africa, she explains, socioeconomic inequalities have inten-
    sified even as people have gained civil and political rights. This is in line with the
    current emphasis on first generation rights that I highlighted above. For Miraftab,
    it is this disjuncture between formal and substantive inclusion that leads to what
    American anthropologist James Holston (2008) calls 'insurgent citizenship' or the
    collective popular protests by informal settlement dwellers to assert their Right to
    the City.

The conflicting nature of access to housing

LEP and Right to the City discourses on housing reflect their distinct ideological differences on the respective roles of state and market. On one hand, the LEP approach emphasises the importance of property formalisation and market inclusion in addressing poor living conditions and vulnerability to eviction in informal settlements. However, it also sees the state and market as mutually reinforcing. The state has an initiating role by facilitating access to housing ownership and thereby reinforcing property rights. In turn, property rights can increase state revenue through taxation, which will enhance its capacity for social provision. On the other hand, the Right to the City presents access to affordable housing as a human right, which should be at the centre of the state's public policy. Instead of viewing market integration as a solution, it highlights the negative effects of market competition on the housing sector in urban Africa.

These two divergent approaches to housing in urban Africa illustrate the conflicting nature of the housing sector in general. As Bengtsson (2001: 257) explains, in all modern welfare societies, 'housing is *at the same time* defined as an individual market commodity and as a public good demanding state involvement'. In that sense, as housing is 'always provided through markets' it is different from other social sectors that are mainly provided through state allocations (Bengtsson 2001). It is therefore not surprising to see the LEP approach, principally influenced by liberal ideas, stressing the market character of housing, while the more social-oriented Right to the City emphasises its character as a public good.

However, despite their different ideological backgrounds, their policy recommendations are not necessarily incompatible. This research has shown that, depending on the advocates, the two discourses have evolved. Their arguments are not fixed, but are adapted across time and place, and are not necessarily always in contradiction. Some arguments put forward by CLEP and by African social movements regarding housing are not in opposition. For example, the policies to facilitate house ownership among people living in poverty and put forward by the LEP report do not contradict the call for access to well-located and affordable housing by African advocates of the Right to the City. In addition, both schools promote collective forms of ownership and land use.

Concluding remarks

In this paper, I have compared the major arguments of the LEP and the Right to the City discourses by focusing on their approach to the issue of housing in urban Africa. I have argued that the discourses are based on two distinct sets of ideological and normative principles, with LEP being inspired by classical liberal ideas and the Right to the City by Marxist thought. Consistent with their different ideological backgrounds, the two discourses suggest two different sets of development policies, with LEP emphasising the role of individual property rights and the Right to the City stressing collective and public services. These contrasting approaches also translate into different views on access to housing in urban Africa. A schematic summary would note that LEP discourse views the market as a solution to lack of access to adequate and affordable housing in African cities, while the Right to the City considers the market as a problem and calls for increased state intervention in housing provision. The policy recommendations of these two discourses reflect these divergent views. However, despite the different ideological backgrounds, some policy recommendations may converge, as in the case of collective ownership.

It must also be recognised that those putting forward the two discourses do not have equal influence. While the CLEP was made up of internationally recognised experts and policy-makers, the Right to the City grassroots organisations and academics whose work I examined have significantly less power and influence. Even though the follow-up on CLEP and the commitments to implement the LEP agenda remain to be seen, the arguments CLEP puts forward are more in line with the dominant market-led vision of development.

Another major finding of this analysis of LEP and the Right to the City is that both discourses have significantly departed from their original meanings. The CLEP Report moved beyond de Soto's liberal focus on property rights formalisation to adopt a broader view, considering legal empowerment as a global social contract involving a so-called 'bundle of rights', including labour rights. Similarly, many current advocates of the Right to the City see it as a call for respect for recognised human rights rather than as a demand for the radical societal transformation envisaged by Lefebvre. Moreover, UN agencies have engaged in promotion of both discourses – with the UNDP hosting CLEP and UN-HABITAT and UNESCO supporting the Right to the City campaign. This may suggest that each discourse has been mainstreamed and diluted to fit the UN framework. By losing their original meaning, concepts can become blurred or all-encompassing. Because discourses evolve and are adapted according to the characteristics of their advocates, it is particularly important to undertake in-depth analyses of development discourse in order to understand its origin and evolution and its policy assessments. In that sense, such analyses are relevant not only to academic debate but also to policy-makers needing to gain a good understanding of these two discourses and their policy implementation.

Consequently, a natural sequel to this research would be examining how the two discourses are implemented in existing policy. Particular cases of housing policy in African cities could be investigated to find out whether and how they invoke the two discourses. The analysis of existing policies may reveal that one discourse is dominant in a particular context. It may also be the case that arguments from both discourses are combined in a single policy.

My focus on the housing sector in urban Africa has certainly influenced the results of my research. First, as noted above, the housing sector is simultaneously defined as an individual market commodity and as a public good demanding state involvement, a contradiction that is at the centre of the analysis in both discourses. It would also be interesting to examine LEP and Right to the City discourses on other social sectors, such as access to water and sanitation, where a greater state role is widely accepted. Second, it would be relevant to look at the two discourses regarding the housing sector in different geographical contexts. Without doubt, the challenges faced in African cities are not the same as those faced by Latin-American and Asian city dwellers. Finally, other approaches focusing on different actors would certainly bring different results. For example, one could look solely at UN-related documents. A comparison of UNDP's view of LEP and UN-HABITAT's of the Right to the City may reveal different aspects of the two discourses.

References

Afenah, A. (2010) 'Reclaiming Citizenship Rights in Accra, Ghana', in A. Sungranyes and C. Mathivet (eds), *Cities for All: Proposals and Experiences toward the Right to the City*, Santiago: Habitat International Coalition, pp. 155–68.

ANLEP (2011) 'Academic Network on Legal Empowerment of the Poor' http://www.sum.uio.no/research/poverty/anlep/index.html (accessed 25 May 2011).

Banik, D. (2009) 'Legal Empowerment as a Conceptual and Operational Tool in Poverty Eradication', *Hague Journal on the Rule of Law*, Vol. 1: 117–31.

Bengtsson, B. (2001) 'Housing as a Social Right: Implications for Welfare State', *Theory Scandinavian Political Studies*, Vol. 24(4): 255–75.

Bradlow, B. (2010) 'Out of the Garden of Eden: Moving beyond the Rights-Based Agenda in the Urban Sector', *Sustainable Development Law and Policy*, Vol. XI(1): 47–71.

Brown, A. and A. Kristiansen (2009) 'Urban Policies and the Right to the City: Rights, responsibilities and citizenship', Paris: UNESCO, UN-HABITAT.

CLEP (2008) *Making the Law Work for Everyone: Volume I Report of the Commission on Legal Empowerment of the Poor*, NY: UNDP.

COHRE (2006) *Global Survey on Forced Evictions: Violations of Human Rights 2003–2006*, Geneva: COHRE.

Costes, L. (2010) 'Le *Droit à la ville* de Henri Lefebvre: quel héritage politique et scientifique ?', *Espaces et Sociétés*, Vol. 1–2(140–1): 177–91.

Davis, M. (2004) 'Planet of Slums: Urban Involution and the Informal Proletariat', *New Left Review*, Vol. 26: 5–34.

De Bruijn, R. (2010) 'The Poor Have the Right to be Housed in Well Located Land', available at: http://abahlali.org/node/6750 (accessed 25 May 2011).

De Soto, H. (2001) 'Dead Capital and the Poor', *SAIS Review*, Vol. XXI(1): 13–43.

De Soto, H. (2000) *The Mystery of Capital: Why Capitalism Triumphs in the West and Fails Everywhere Else*, London: Bantam.

De Soto, H. (1989) *The other path: The invisible revolution in the Third World*, London: Tauris.

Du Plessis, J. (2005) 'The growing problem of forced evictions and the crucial importance of community-based, locally appropriated alternatives', *Environment and Urbanization,* Vol. 17(1): 123–34.

Eyben, R. and R. Napier-Moore (2009) 'Choosing Words with Care? Shifting meanings of women's empowerment in international development', *Third World Quarterly,* Vol. 30(2): 285–300.

Faundez, J. (2009) 'Empowering workers in the informal economy', *Hague Journal on the Rule of Law*, Vol. 1(1): 156–72.

Fumtim, J. (2010) 'Building Cities for and by the People: The Right to the City in Africa', in A. Sungranyes and C. Mathivet (eds), *Cities for All: Proposals and Experiences toward the Right to the City,* Santiago: Habitat International Coalition, 195–200.

Friedmann, J. (1995) 'The Right to the City', *Society and Nature,* Vol. 1(1): 71–84.

Gilbert, A. (2002) 'On the mystery of capital and the myths of Hernando de Soto', *International Development Policy Review,* Vol. 24 (1): 1–19.

Golub, S. (2003) *Beyond Rule of Law Orthodoxy: The Legal Empowerment Alternative,* Working Paper No. 41, Rule of Law Series, Washington DC: Carnegie Endowment for International Peace.

Green, D. (2008) *From Poverty to Power: How active citizens and effective states can change the world,* Oxford: Oxfam International.

Hart, K. (1979) 'Informal Income Opportunities and Urban Employment in Ghana', Journal of Modern African Studies, Vol. 11(1): 61–89.

Harvey, D. (2008) 'The Right to the City', *New Left Review,* Vol. 53: 23–40.

Hirschl, R. (2000) 'Negative Rights vs. Positive Entitlements: A Comparative Study of Judicial Interpretations of Rights in an Emerging Neo-Liberal Economic Order', *Human Rights Quarterly*, Vol. 22: 1060–98.

Holston, J. (2008) *Insurgent Citizenship: Disjunctions of Democracy and Modernity in Brazil,* Princeton: Princeton University Press.

Huchzermeyer, M. (2010) 'The Policy Context for Informal Settlements: Competitiveness, Slum Eradication and a Right to the City?', *Trialog,* Vol. 104(1): 25–8.

ILD (2011) 'Our history', available at: http://www.ild.org.pe/ (accessed 25 May 2011).

Joireman, S.F. (2008) 'The Mystery of Capital Formation in sub-Saharan Africa: Women, Property Rights and Customary Law', *World Development*, Vol. 36(7): 1233–46.

Jones, P. (1994) *Rights*, Houndmills Basingstoke: Palgrave.

Kabeer, N. (2002) 'Reflections on the Measurement of Women's Empowerment', *Discussing Women's Empowerment: Theory and Practice*, Sida Studies No.3, 17–58.

Lees, L. (2004) 'Urban geography: Discourse analysis and urban research', *Progress in Human Geography*, Vol. 28(1), 101–7.

Lefebvre, H. (1996) *Writings on Cities*, Oxford: Blackwell.

Lindell, I., M. Hedman and K. Nathan-Verboomen (2010) 'The World Cup 2010 and the urban poor: "World class cities" for all?', Policy Note No. 5. Uppsala: Nordic Africa Institute.

Lopes de Souza, M. (2010) '*Which* right to *which* city? In defence of political-strategical clarity', *Interface*, Vol. 2(1): 315–33.

Mayer, M. (2009) 'The "Right to the City" in the context of shifting mottos of urban social movements', *City*, Vol. 13(2-3): 362–74.

Mathivet, C. and S. Buckingham (2009) 'The Abahlali baseMjondolo Shack Dwellers Movement and the Right to the City in South Africa', available at: http://base.d-p-h.info/en/fiches/dph/fiche-dph-8059.html (accessed 25 May 2011).

Miraftab, F. (2009) 'Insurgent Planning: Situating Radical Planning in the Global South', *Planning Theory*, Vol. 8(1): 32–50.

Ortiz, E. (2010) 'The Construction Process towards the Right to the City: Progress made and challenges pending' in A. Sungranyes and C. Mathivet (eds), *Cities for All: Proposals and Experiences toward the Right to the City*, Santiago: Habitat International Coalition, 113–20.

Parnell, S. and E. Pieterse (2010) 'The "Right to the City": Institutional Imperatives of a Developmental State', *International Journal of Urban and Regional Research*, Vol. 34(1): 146–62.

Payne, G., A. Durand-Lasserve and C. Rakodi (2009) 'The limits of land titling and home ownership', *Environment and Urbanization*, Vol. 21(2): 443–62.

Pithouse, R. (2010) 'Local Despotisms and the Limits of the Discourse of "Delivery" in South Africa', *Trialog*, Vol. 204(1): 48–55.

Purcell, M. (2006) 'Urban Democracy and the Local Trap', *Urban Studies*, Vol. 43(11): 1921–41.

Purcell, M. (2002) 'Excavating Lefebvre: The right to the city and its urban politics of the inhabitant', *GeoJournal*, Vol. 58: 99–108.

Royston, L. (2006) 'Barking dogs and building bridges: A contribution to making sense of Hernando de Soto's ideas in the South African context', in M. Huchzermeyer and A. Karam (eds), *Informal Settlements: a Perpetual Challenge?*, Cape Town: UCT Press, 165–79.

Sassen, S. (1996) 'Whose City Is It? Globalization and the Formation of New Claims', *Public Culture*, Vol. 8: 205–23.

Soja, E.W. (1995) 'Editiorial', *Society and Space*, Vol. 9: 257–9.

Stephens, M. (2009) 'The Commission on Legal Empowerment of the Poor: An Opportunity Missed', *Hague Journal on the Rule of Law*, Vol. 1: 132–57.

Unger, K. (2009) '"Right to the City" as a response to the crisis: "convergence" or divergence of urban social movements?', available at: http://www.reclaiming-spaces.org/crisis/archives/266 (accessed 25 May 2011)

UN-HABITAT, UNEP (2010) *State of African Cities 2010: Governance, Inequality and Urban Land Markets*, London: UN-HABITAT, UNEP.

UN-HABITAT (2008) *State of the World Cities 2010/2011: Bridging the Urban Divide*, London: UN-HABITAT.

Van Boven, T. C. (1979) 'Distinguishing criteria of Human Rights' in K. Vasak (ed.), *The International Dimensions of Human Rights*, Paris: UNESCO, 41–58.

Varley, A. (2002) 'Private or Public: Debating the meaning of tenure legalization', *International Journal of Urban and Regional Research*, Vol. 26(3): 449–61.

World Charter on the Right to the City (2005), available at: http://www.urbanre-inventors.net/3/wsf.pdf (accessed 15 May 2011).

About the author

Louisa Vogiazides, has a master's degree from the Department of Human Geography at Stockholm University and a master's in International Politics from the University of Manchester. Her research interests are development, urbanization and migration issues. She has also worked as a Policy Assistant at Eurostep, a Brussels-based development NGO.